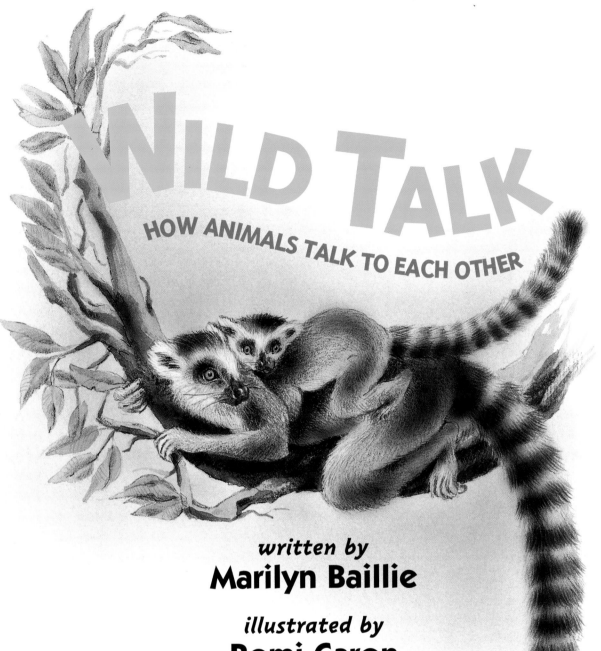

WILD TALK

HOW ANIMALS TALK TO EACH OTHER

written by
Marilyn Baillie

illustrated by
Romi Caron

Owl Books

Owl Books are published by Greey de Pencier Books Inc.,
179 John Street, Suite 500, Toronto, Ontario M5T 3G5

OWL and the Owl colophon are trademarks of Owl Communications.
Greey de Pencier Books Inc. is a licensed user of trademarks of Owl Communications.

Distributed in the United States by Firefly Books (U.S.) Inc.,
230 Fifth Avenue, Suite 1607, New York, NY 10001.

This book was published with the generous support of the Canada Council,
the Ontario Arts Council and the Ontario Publishing Centre.

Consultant
Katherine E. Wynne-Edwards, PhD, Biology Dept., Queen's University, Kingston, Ontario

Dedication
For Farideh de Bosset

Author Acknowledgements
A special thank-you to Dr. Katherine Wynne-Edwards for her expertise and generous assistance.
A big thank-you to Editor-in-Chief Sheba Meland and editor Kat Mototsune for their energy and enthusiasm,
to Julia Naimska for her creative design and to Romi Caron for her engaging illustrations.

Canadian Cataloguing in Publication Data
Baillie, Marilyn
Wild talk : how animals talk to each other

(Amazing things animals do)
ISBN 1-895688-54-X (bound) ISBN 1-895688-55-8 (pbk.)

1. Animal communication – Juvenile literature.
I. Caron, Romi. II. Title. III. Series: Baillie,
Marilyn. Amazing things animals do.

QL776.B35 1996   j591.59   C95-932570-0

Design & Art Direction: Julia Naimska

Photo credits: p. 6, Wolfgang Bayer/Bruce Coleman Inc.; pp. 8, 14, 16, 20, 22, 26, J.D. Taylor;
p. 10, Gerard Lacz/Peter Arnold, Inc.; p. 12, John M. Burnley/Bruce Coleman Inc.;
p. 18, Arthur Strange/Valan Photos; p. 24, Wayne Lankinen/Valan Photos;
p. 28, J.A. Wilkinson/Valan Photos; pp. 30 – 31 as above.

Printed in Hong Kong

A   B   C   D   E   F

Contents

ANIMAL TALK

How do you talk to other people? You can speak, shout, whisper or use hand signals to get your message across. You can smile or frown, or hug someone to let them know how you feel. You can teach someone something by showing them what to do. People understand by watching and listening to you. Animals have a lot to say to each other, too. They don't use words. They use special signals and signs for other animals to see, hear, smell or feel.

How do animals talk to each other? To find mates, tiny fireflies signal with light and cranes dance. To feel close to others in their families, elephants rumble and chimpanzees touch. Howler monkeys roar and ring-tailed lemurs leave their scent to keep others away. Great frigate birds do things over and over again to teach their young how to act. Humpback whales sing, but no one is exactly sure why.

Wolves sometimes "speak" with the looks on their faces and the way they sit or stand. From the time they are very young, baby wolves watch their parents and then copy their actions while they play. Look carefully at the wolf pups playing in this picture. Can you tell which one is acting angry, which one is acting hungry, which one feels left out and which one wants to play? (Answers are on page 32.) Now turn the pages and let some animals talk to you.

HIGH-UP HOWLING

A roar jolts the sleeping rain forest just as the sun comes up. "Aaarrooo-oo-oo-gaaahhh!" A howler monkey greets the day with his booming howl. Soon, all the howler monkeys in the troop join in the leader's noisy call. The big voice box in the throat of a howler monkey makes deep, loud roars. The males have the largest voice boxes and the deepest calls.

One by one, the males, females and babies follow the leader as he moves through the treetops. In a long line they search for figs, flowers or nuts to eat. But look, there are other howler monkeys nearby! The howlers start roaring again. "Get away!" they seem to say, "You can't have the food from our trees." All day they guard their part of the forest from the other howler monkeys. And, when the sun goes down, they all roar together once more before going to sleep high in the treetops.

6

Dance with Me

Two Japanese cranes, a male and a female, greet each other. They face each other and start to dance, casting swaying shadows on the snow. As their graceful wings unfold, they bend and bow. Suddenly, the male springs up into the air. Up, up, again and again he jumps. The female watches him and dances around him. Then it's her turn to dance as he watches.

Soon other cranes in the flock find partners and begin to dance, too. The wintering ground is full of dancing cranes. These birds dance to find a mate for life. Together a pair of cranes will hatch eggs into chicks. They will move to other places as the seasons change. They will dance together many times to show how close they are. But this first time, they dance their very best.

SMELLY SIGNALS

A troop of ring-tailed lemurs stops to rest. They touch and clean each other's fur. Sometimes they make soft grunting noises. This is how they say that they all belong together. After a warm bask in the sun, they start to move through the dry Madagascar forest. They hold their long striped tails straight up as they travel. One female lemur leads them as they search for food.

Suddenly the leader stops and does a hand-stand. She brushes her bottom against a low tree branch. As the base of her tail touches the branch, it leaves a smell there. It's a message to other lemur troops that this part of the forest is taken. Each lemur in the troop flips upside-down to leave a message too. But sometimes lemurs from other troops still get too close. Then the males stand up on their hind legs and rub their tails over scent glands on their wrists. Their tails get loaded with smelly musk. On four feet, they move towards the strangers. They quickly flick their tails, sending a smelly warning. Peee-uuu!

NIGHT LIGHTS

Blink, blink . . . flash! A male firefly darts through the warm evening air. He lights up again and again, like a tiny flashlight flicking on and off. His signal is seen by the female fireflies in the grass. Flash! A female lights up at the right time to catch his attention. He zigzags in her direction. Their lights tell each other that they are the same kind of firefly, so they will be perfect mates.

Fireflies carry a built-in lantern in their bodies. The cold, greenish glow is made by special chemicals inside the firefly. Each kind of firefly has its own special code. The code is made up of flashes of light, quick and slow, bright and dim. That's how a hungry female firefly can fool a male of another kind of firefly. She blinks back his signal and waits for him to fly down. Then, to his surprise, he becomes a meal instead of a mate. Blink, blink . . . glub!

12

WARNING WHINNY

Zebras peacefully munch on grasses, side by side with antelopes. There is safety in numbers for all the animals. "Ee-aa, ee-aa," a zebra mare neighs softly to keep in touch with her foal. Zebras know each other by voice, stripe pattern and scent. They sniff the breeze for the smell of danger. Suddenly, their ears twitch forward and their nostrils quiver. They are on the alert.

A lioness is creeping through the long grass. A large zebra stallion barks a loud warning, "Danger! Gallop away!" In the dust of stamping hooves, zebra families come together. A mare leads the escape. The foals and other mares in her family follow. The strong stallion protects from the back of the group. A mass of black and white stripes streaks across the African plains to safety.

LEADER OF THE PACK

"Ahoooooo! Ahoooooo!" The wolf howl fills the forest. Other wolves in the pack throw back their heads and join their leader in his howling. The howl calls them together as they get ready to hunt. Wolves also howl after eating, and to talk to each other over long distances. A lonely howl might mean that a male is starting his own pack and is looking for wolves to run with him.

Each wolf has a special place in the wolf pack. All the wolves obey the leader. He holds his tail high and fluffs out his fur to tell the others that he is in command. Another wolf flattens his ears and tucks in his tail, whines and licks the leader's muzzle, signalling, "You are our chief." And if the wolves forget who is in charge, the leader reminds them with a glare, an angry face and bared teeth. The pups in the pack watch carefully. Their parents teach them by example, so they will learn their place in the pack.

As the wolves move through the woods, they leave urine markings on trees. The smell tells other wolves who has been here and how long ago. Wolves mark all around their territory to keep other wolf packs away. The pack will need all the food in this area to survive.

SEEING RED

Is that a bright red balloon in the branches? No, it's a male great frigate bird. He has a colorful way to signal that he is looking for a mate. His fire-red throat pouch puffs out, shining in the Galapagos sun. He shows off, flapping his wings and clacking his bill. Finally, a female arrives to be his partner. They build a nest of twigs and hatch one white egg into a chick.

Great frigate birds are fantastic fliers. Fast and smooth, they dip and soar in the air. The parents must teach their chick how to hunt on the wing, so both parents show the chick over and over again. First they show it how to swoop down on sticks and feathers. Once the chick can grab floating sticks from the air, it tries for fish near the surface of the ocean. Great frigate birds cannot dive into the sea to catch fish, so the chick must learn to get close to the food on the top of the water. Its parents teach it to fly so well, it can even snatch food on the wing from other birds.

Deep Sea Songs

Deep groans and high whistles, loud roars and soft sighs — the ocean is full of whale music. The songs of the humpback whales echo through the water. "Sigh . . . squawk, chirp, groan . . . roar!" Male humpbacks swim in a group. Each whale sings almost the same song, and their voices flow together. As they chant, their song changes during the long voyage. From the cold Arctic ocean they glide to warm breeding waters. They sing the most here, where the humpback cows and calves gather.

What messages are the whales sending? Nobody really knows. The male whales sing near the females. Are they singing for a mate? The humpbacks sing on long swims through the ocean. Are they telling other whales where they are? Are they warning away others from where they feed? There is so much more for us to learn about these singing giants.

CHIMP CHATTER

Two young chimpanzees play on the forest floor, rolling and tickling. When the baby flops into their mother's lap, she holds and strokes him. He whimpers and pouts at his big sister, who pats at his back and snuggles beside him. The mother chimpanzee gently cleans her children's fur. The family uses play and touching and sound to say how close they feel.

Other chimpanzees appear through the leafy bushes. Their soft cries of pleasure and excited faces show they are friends. Both these families belong to the same chimpanzee group. Chimpanzees in the group talk to each other in many ways. They loudly call and hoot to keep in touch over long distances. Their faces show if they are angry, happy, afraid or surprised. Their hands reach out to ask for something, to make friends, or to shoo another chimpanzee away. The adults in the group protect this area of the forest. If outsiders come too close, they run at them with their arms stretched high and bark an angry "Wraa!"

22

SERENADE IN BLUE

"Chur-wi, chur-wi, chur-wi," the bluebird warbles from the top of a fence. He has shed his old feathers, and his new ones shimmer in the morning sun. His mate admires his sky-blue feathers and his lilting love song. He flies across the spring green field to her, carrying a juicy grasshopper as a gift. He feeds it to her to let her know that it's time to build a nest and lay eggs.

Soon the eggs hatch into hungry nestlings. The bright yellow of their gaping mouths tells the parents what the babies want. "Feed me, feed me!" they squawk and chirp. Their parents take turns feeding the chicks. They fly far to find insects for the young to eat. At last the father bluebird rests on a branch outside his home. "Chur-wi, chur-wi, chur-wi," he calls. He tells the other birds that this is where his family is, so stay away.

LONG DISTANCE CALL

Trekking across the African plain, a herd of elephants stops suddenly. The female elephants and calves that make up the herd stand very still. They all face the same direction, and lift their large ears to listen. There isn't a sound to be heard by you or me. But the elephants are getting a deep, rumbling message from far away. It's another elephant herd, travelling in the same direction.

The elephants answer with the same rumbling sounds from the base of their trunks. The rumbles are loud and travel a long way. But they are too deep for human ears to hear. Groups of elephants use the rumbles to keep in touch as they travel. Males and females also rumble to each other across vast distances. When a female is ready to mate, she sends a message far and wide. Male elephants, roaming alone, hear her and know where to find her. They follow her call and fight for her attention.

Elephants have many other ways of talking to each other. They snort, trumpet, touch trunks and turn in circles. By smell and touch and sound, they greet each other and stay close in their groups. But for long-distance messages, elephants use the deep, low rumbling to talk across the plains.

FROGGY EVENING

All through the day, the bullfrog floats in the water near the edge of the pond. Once in a while, he catches a dragonfly with his swift tongue. Without a sound, he waits for night to fall. When tall bullrushes and reeds finally cast moon shadows on the pond, he starts to sing in a great, booming voice. "Aurumph, aurumph, aurumph," he croaks into the cool spring night.

After a silent winter, why is the bullfrog singing now? When the spring sun makes the pond water warm enough, the bullfrog knows it's time to find a mate. He forces air past his windpipe to make a croak. A sac of loose skin at his throat starts to puff out like a balloon. The sound will echo in this sac and boom past the pond and over the meadow. He is announcing to the world that he is looking for a female. He tells other males that this is his area in the pond, so stay out. If a female bullfrog likes his song, they will mate. Soon the bullfrog will be silent again, and the pond will be full of baby frogs called tadpoles.

Who's Who

Red Howler Monkey

Howler monkeys live in tropical forests and range from southern Mexico through Central America, to northern Argentina in South America. They can have red, black or brown fur, and they all use their prehensile tails to cling to branches. They are the size of a medium-sized dog.

Firefly

Fireflies live in woods and meadows, near streams and even in back yards. There are more than 130 species or types of fireflies around the world, each with its own light code. A firefly is a bit longer than a housefly, but all you would notice is a quick, bright flash if you saw one at night.

Japanese Crane

Japanese or Manchurian cranes are a symbol of love, happiness and long life in Japan. Their graceful shapes are used on clothing and artwork. They are the largest cranes in Japan and live on the northern island of Hokkaido. Tall and elegant, they are about the height of a twelve-year-old child.

Zebra

A zebra looks like a horse with black and white stripes. There are three kinds of zebras, and they all live in Africa. Although all zebras have stripes, no two zebras have exactly the same stripe pattern. Zebras are often found in mixed herds along with antelopes or wildebeest.

Ring-tailed Lemur

All lemurs live in Madagascar, off the coast of Africa. Ring-tailed lemurs live in the dry southern forests of this big island. During the day, they travel in troops of up to 25, and at night they curl up together to keep warm. An adult is the size of a large housecat, but has a much longer tail.

Wolf

Wolves are related to dogs, but are bigger and have longer legs. Gray or Timber wolves can range in color from black to white. They live in packs in northern North America and Eurasia, preferring open forests and tundra. The leader of the pack and his mate are called the alpha male and female.

GREAT FRIGATE BIRD

Frigate birds nest on tropical islands, such as the Galapagos Islands off the coast of South America. Their wide wingspans and light bodies make these sea birds agile fliers. They can even steal food from other birds in midair. A frigate bird's wingspan is about as far as you and a friend could stretch out your arms side by side.

EASTERN BLUEBIRD

Look in orchards and open farmland in North America and you might see a bluebird. The Eastern bluebird is a little longer than your outstretched hand, and is bright blue with an orangey chest. Some bluebirds' natural nesting sites were taken over by house sparrows and starlings, so people have set up nest boxes for them to use.

HUMPBACK WHALE

Humpback whales migrate through the oceans from the polar waters to the tropical seas. They are huge but agile, leaping out of the waves and slapping the surface of the water with their wide tails as they dive back in. A humpback whale is about as long as two school buses parked end to end.

AFRICAN ELEPHANT

You can find African elephants in the forest and open savannah areas of Africa. The low, rumbling sound that they send over long distances comes from the area where their trunks meet their foreheads. It is called infrasound. Infrasound is also in wind, thunder and ocean storms, but we can't hear it.

CHIMPANZEE

Chimpanzees are found throughout west, central and east Africa, wherever there are rain forests, mountain forests and savannah woodlands. Just like humans, chimpanzees show various facial expressions, and they are our closest living animal relatives. An adult chimpanzee is just a little shorter than the average human.

BULLFROG

Home for the American bullfrog is in the lakes and ponds of North America. It is the largest species of frog in North America, and has the loudest croak. An adult bullfrog with its legs outstretched is about the length of a tall drinking glass. When fully inflated, the male's throat sac can be half again as big as the whole frog.

WHO AM I?

Here's a quiz for you to try. Each clue tells you how an animal talks to the others of its kind. Which animal is speaking?

1 My low rumbles travel far to send messages across the African plains.

2 I sing sweetly to my mate and give her insects as presents. Then I sing a warning to others to stay out of my home.

3 In our group, we often touch and gesture to talk to each other. And when an intruder comes near, an adult will charge and yell to scare it away.

4 I puff up my fire-red pouch to show a female I want her to be my partner.

5 I croak into the spring evening to say that this part of the pond is mine.

6 I light up and blink a flashy message at night.

7 I sing mysterious songs as I glide through the open ocean.

8 I do a handstand with my tail in the air to leave scent messages on a tree.

9 I am patterned with stripes, and neigh a warning to others when danger is near.

10 I spring high in the air to dance and to tell my partner we'll be together for life.

11 My big voice box makes a loud roar that echoes through the treetops.

12 I live in a group, with a leader whose angry glare and growl tells me to behave.

ANSWERS

Animal Talk, p. 5: The wolf pup on the left is touching its nose to its mother's mouth to nuzzle for food; the black wolf pup showing its teeth is acting angry; the wolf pup with its head down and tail up wants to play; and the wolf pup on the right is howling because it feels lonely.

Who Am I? p. 32: 1. African Elephant; **2.** Eastern Bluebird; **3.** Chimpanzee; **4.** Great Frigate Bird; **5.** Bullfrog; **6.** Firefly; **7.** Humpback Whale; **8.** Ring-tailed Lemur; **9.** Zebra; **10.** Japanese Crane; **11.** Red Howler Monkey; **12.** Wolf.